A Sunshine Day!
A Kid's Guide To Willemstad, Curacao

Photography by John D. Weigand
Poetry by Penelope Dyan

Bellissima Publishing, LLC
Jamul, California
www.bellissimapublishing.com

Copyright © 2019 by Penny D. Weigand & John D. Weigand

All rights reserved. No part of this book may be reproduced or transmitted in any form or by any means, electronic or mechanical, including photocopying, recording, or by any other means, or by any information or storage retrieval system, without permission from the publisher.

ISBN 978-1-61477-384-9
First Edition

"Life is full of surprises, both big and small. The trick is to recognize them all!"

PENELOPE DYAN

A Sunshine Day!
Bellissima Publishing, LLC

Introduction

Willemstad, capital city of Curacao, sits an sunny island in the southern Caribbean Sea. Its stylistic Dutch touch comes from being one of the ABC islands, a part of Netherlands Antilles. This UNESCO World Heritage City is a fun place to visit. Its brightly painted Dutch colonial houses, waterfront, and the pontoon bridge over St. Anna Bay, and RIF fort, all contribute to the scene. There are places you can shop; and the moving pontoon bridge is an adventure all of its own, if it just happens to move just as you happen to step off of it, or while you are crossing it!

Use this fun, 'learn to read' book filled with word repetition, word recognition and rhyme to practice reading skills and to get a kid's eye view of what a kid will see when they visit the city of Curacao! Then get ready for some 'Caribbean-Dutch' fun! And, of course, because this is an Island, there are lots of great beaches, not to mention the warm Caribbean sun!

For even more learning fun, go to Bellissimavideo's YouTube Channel, and watch the free music video that goes with this book! And remember to have fun learning! Because if a kid doesn't have fun learning, a kid won't love to learn!

A Sunshine Day!
Bellissima Publishing, LLC

A Sunshine Day!
A Kid's Guide To Willemstad, Curacao

Photography by John D. Weigand
Poetry by Penelope Dyan

You can come here by plane;
but if you come here by boat,
right into the port of Willemstad,
(the capital of Curacao)
you will happily float!

You see a boat
and colorful Dutch buildings galore!
Mom says happily,
"Soon you will see even MORE!"
Dad smiles and rubs his eyes.
You ALL look ahead.
You are all kind of tired,
because you just got out of BED!

You get off the ship.
You walk along, and then you all stop.
Mom takes a deep breath;
and she says,
"I just HAVE to SHOP!"
Mom buys you each a bag and a hat.
She says,
"I'm all done with shopping!"
Dad says,
"We'll see about THAT!""

Then you see a giant wooden shoe!
It's way too big for a kid
the size of YOU!

You see a giant pink flamingo!
You see a whimsical whale!
You see A LOT of other STUFF!
AND you look all around
until you've seen ENOUGH!

You see two cannons.
Sis counts them out loud,
"One cannon! Two!"
She says,
"There is one for me!
And there is one for you!"

You and Sis laugh.
And you decide to explore!
Mom tells you to keep moving along,
because THEN . . .
you will see even MORE!

And THEN you see a pontoon bridge!
And it is REALLY, REALLY neat!
But Mom starts to worry
when it moves . . .
because it MOVES . . .
right beneath HER two FEET!

You hurry to the OTHER side.
And THEN you all stop for a SNACK!
And when you are done snacking,
you take the ferry BACK!

You see a bright orange building.
Mom says,
"What a colorful sight!"
Dad says it is built in the Dutch style,
AND Mom agrees that he is RIGHT!

And next you see a building
that is BOTH orange AND blue;
and Dad knowingly exclaims,
"That's in the Dutch style TOO!"

And then . . . oh so sadly
(as you ALL oh so sadly know)
Dad oh so sadly announces,
"I'm afraid it is time to go!"
And so you all head back,
and you hop aboard your boat!
And toward the Panama Canal
you all NOW oh so HAPPILY float!
And THAT night,
as you lie in your bed,
you think all about the adventures
that for you
oh so HAPPILY lie ahead!

"All of Life is one great big adventure!"

PENELOPE DYAN

www.ingramcontent.com/pod-product-compliance
Ingram Content Group UK Ltd.
Pitfield, Milton Keynes, MK11 3LW, UK
UKHW060132240426
12048UKWH00002B/7